This book is a work of non-fiction. Every reasonable effort has been made to ensure accuracy, but names, facts, dates, and quotations have been carefully verified to the best of the author's ability. Any errors or omissions are unintentional.

Cover design, layout, and internal formatting by the author.
Published independently in 2025.

BORNA AHADI
bornaahadi@gmail.com

CONTENTS

DARK HEIR

Kim Yo-jong and the Future of North Korea

Borna Ahadi

INTRODUCTION

In the mid-1990s, two children from East Asia stood wide-eyed before the gates of Disneyland Paris, indistinguishable from the throngs of European tourists surrounding them. Their small hands clutched cotton candy, their laughter indistinct from the chorus of delight echoing through the park. They marveled at the glimmering turrets of Sleeping Beauty's castle, unaware—or perhaps far too aware—that they were not like the others. The names on their passports were false. Their smiles, rehearsed. And their future, meticulously scripted by one of the world's most secretive regimes. These were no ordinary siblings. They were Kim Jong-un and Kim Yo-jong—the shadow prince and the ghost princess of North Korea.

She was the younger of the two. A girl born into silence, molded by secrecy. Her childhood was cloaked in aliases and European boarding schools, her lineage veiled behind diplomatic covers. In Switzerland, classmates saw a quiet, well-behaved girl with an inscrutable gaze. Few suspected that behind that mask was a living heir to a dynasty forged in blood and isolation. Fewer still imagined that she, not her brother, would one day emerge as the most enigmatic and potentially dangerous figure in the Kim lineage. She was always there, always present, yet forever out of focus—an accessory in official narratives, a shadow gliding behind the family's myth.

Kim Yo-jong was not destined to rule. She was not groomed in the traditional sense. North Korea was a patriarchy wrapped in ideology, its throne passed from grandfather to father to son. But history, in its penchant for irony, often selects its own instruments of disruption. And in a land of crumbling icons and decaying myths, a new face emerged from the wings—subtle, calculating, and terrifyingly competent. She did not take power with a fist, but with a whisper. She did not conquer headlines with fire, but with silence.

From her earliest roles in the Propaganda and Agitation Department, Yo-jong proved herself indispensable to her brother's image. While Kim Jong-un performed the theater of leadership, it was Yo-jong who designed the stage. She controlled the lighting. She rewrote the script. She softened his image when the world saw a volatile tyrant and sharpened it when strength was needed. Her fingerprints were on every broadcast, every photograph, every speech. She managed not just information, but perception. If North Korea's dictatorship had an architect in the 21st century, it was her—deft with illusion, merciless in narrative warfare.

The world first glimpsed her face in February 2018 at the Winter Olympics in Pyeongchang. There she sat, composed and elegant, across the arena from U.S. Vice President Mike Pence. For a fleeting moment, she embodied a possibility unthinkable for decades: a thaw in the eternal freeze of Korean conflict. Yet, beneath that diplomatic facade lay the same DNA that ordered purges, executions, and provocations. She was never merely a messenger of peace. She was an emissary of calculation. She appeared disarming, dispassionate, and calm—but hers was the kind of calm that precedes chaos.

As her brother's health faltered and international rumors swirled about his potential demise, attention turned to her. There was no male heir apparent. No trusted inner circle member with her loyalty or clarity of vision. And so, she stepped further into the light—not with declarations or military parades, but with statements sharp as daggers and decisions that left diplomats scrambling. She called South Korea "a barking dog" and laughed at Western sanctions. She orchestrated balloon warfare and digital propaganda campaigns. Where her brother wielded power like a club, she preferred the scalpel. Her provocations came wrapped in diplomatic syntax, her threats folded in velvet.

Kim Yo-jong is not a curiosity. She is not a novelty. She is the product of a regime that has learned to evolve while appearing stagnant, to smile while drawing blood. And she is perhaps the only figure within the Kim dynasty who truly understands the 21st-century battlefield—not just nuclear brinkmanship, but narrative warfare, image manipulation, and the politics of ambiguity. Her rise is not just a story of dynastic intrigue, but a harbinger of the future of authoritarianism itself. She represents the synthesis of two eras—the old-world secrecy of Cold War communism and the digital sleight-of-hand of contemporary autocracy.

This book is not a biography in the traditional sense. It is an excavation. A journey through the mirrors and mazes of a regime that thrives on misdirection, whose most powerful weapon may not be missiles or soldiers, but the woman who commands its image. From the European classrooms of her youth to the halls of Pyongyang's brutalist power structures, we will follow Kim Yo-jong as she ascends—step by step, silence by silence—into the most perilous role on Earth. Her every move cloaked in ambiguity, her every word calibrated to distort. She is the ghost at the feast, the mind behind the mask, the one who whispers where others shout.

There will be no coronation. There may never be an official transfer of power. But make no mistake: the machinery of control is already responding to her hand. While global attention pivots to missile tests and diplomatic summits, she sits at the nerve center of a regime whose greatest export is fear and whose ultimate weapon may not be war—but the woman who knows how to win one without firing a single shot.

The Dark Heir has arrived. And the world has only just begun to see her.

THE CASTLE ON THE HORIZON

In the mid-1990s, nestled among the pastel fantasy architecture of Disneyland Paris, two children from a faraway and forbidden land stood captivated by a world that glittered with innocence. The sun glinted off the gold-tipped spires of Sleeping Beauty's Castle as families swirled around them in an orchestra of joy. These children, a boy and a girl, were dressed like every other tourist child—jeans, sneakers, soft smiles drawn across their youthful faces. But nothing about them was ordinary.

Unbeknownst to the thousands of visitors that day, these were the heirs of one of the world's most brutal regimes. Kim Jong-un and Kim Yo-jong—scions of the ruling Kim family of North Korea—stood at the gates of a place built on imagination, while their lives were mapped out by a harsh reality that few in the park could fathom. Their presence in Europe was cloaked in secrecy. Their names, their origins, even their identities were all concealed under layers of diplomatic subterfuge. Their passports were falsified. Their guardians, posing as East Asian envoys or consular officials, lived under constant surveillance and precaution. But to the children, this was a rare moment of freedom—fleeting, precious, and alien.

The castle loomed large not just in the physical landscape of Disneyland, but in the inner world of Kim Yo-jong. It symbolized something forbidden yet mesmerizing: a life filled with laughter, with open affection, with possibility. And for a brief moment, perhaps she allowed herself to believe that the world was truly like this—filled with music, fairytales, and wide-open doors. But reality was never far behind. In the glitter of the parade floats and the whimsical choreography of Disney characters lay a quiet reminder that her future would not be decided by dreams, but by duty.

The 1990s were a time of enormous upheaval within the Hermit Kingdom. Kim Il-sung, the founding patriarch of North Korea, had passed away in 1994, leaving behind a system teetering on the brink of collapse. His son, Kim Jong-il, assumed power amidst famine, economic ruin, and diplomatic isolation. To shield the youngest members of the family from the turmoil—perhaps even to shape them for the future—they were sent abroad. Switzerland was the choice: neutral, quiet, discreet. And Disneyland became a surreal waypoint on that journey.

But the symbolism of that castle—its fairy-tale perfection, its alluring contradiction to the family's ideological roots—would linger. While Disneyland Paris represented the apex of capitalist whimsy, North Korea was a bastion of Stalinist orthodoxy. While Sleeping Beauty dreamed beneath her tower, North Koreans lived under the waking nightmare of starvation and surveillance. Yo-jong, even as a child, would grow to internalize the dissonance between these worlds. One world gave her a taste of what could be. The other, what had to be.

In her eyes, that castle wasn't just a memory. It was a mirage. A vision of a different fate she would never have. But unlike her brother, whose leadership would embody the aggression and brutality of the dynasty, Kim Yo-jong would learn from that contrast. She would carry it. She would use it. And in time, she would harness its symbolism—not to rebel, but to perfect the illusion. She would become the architect of North Korea's most deceptive campaign: the fantasy of change.

While tourists snapped photos and waved to parading princesses, Yo-jong stared beyond the turrets. What she saw wasn't make-believe. It was potential. She learned, even then, that the power of image could surpass the power of force. That a smile, properly timed, could disarm entire nations. That costumes, stories, and stagecraft could make even the most grotesque realities appear palatable. And as she returned to her hotel that evening, silent and observant, a seed was planted. It would take years to blossom—but it would.

This chapter, though hidden in history, marks the beginning of a strange metamorphosis. The girl who stood beneath the golden spires of a foreign fantasyland would one day craft her own kingdom of illusion—one far more dangerous than Disneyland. Because unlike the fairy tales, hers would be built not on dreams, but on deception. Not on magic, but manipulation.

And her castle would not be one of wonder, but of power.

For Kim Yo-jong, the castle on the horizon was never about escape. It was a mirror. And what she saw staring back from its reflection was the truth she would carry with her into the cold corridors of North Korean politics: appearances are everything, and the best lie is the one wrapped in beauty.

BORN IN THE SHADOWS

She was born in a land where truth is dictated, not discovered—where the sun does not rise unless the Supreme Leader commands it so. The exact year of Kim Yo-jong's birth is itself a mystery, shrouded in conflicting records and purposeful ambiguity. Most sources place her birth between 1987 and 1989, a temporal limbo that reflects the uncertainty surrounding her entire existence. From the moment she entered the world, Kim Yo-jong was a ghost in the making—alive, real, and yet unseen by all but a chosen few.

Her mother, Ko Yong-hui, was not the wife of Kim Jong-il but his consort, a Japanese-born dancer of Korean heritage. This delicate status made Ko and her children politically vulnerable. In a regime obsessed with purity and legitimacy, being the child of a woman born in Japan—a former colonial occupier—was a potential stain. It was a contradiction to be hidden, a flaw to be erased from the record. And so, Kim Yo-jong was tucked away, raised within the inner sanctums of privilege but denied the open acknowledgment granted to male heirs.

While her half-brother Kim Jong-nam, born of a different mother, became a public figure of sorts in the 1990s, Yo-jong was never presented to the North Korean people. There were no photographs, no formal declarations, no celebrations of her birth. Her very identity was a state secret, carefully buried beneath layers of disinformation. To outsiders, she did not exist. To insiders, she was part of a hidden strategy—a contingency plan for a future no one dared to predict.

From the outset, her life was one of contradiction. She was born into unimaginable privilege—palatial residences, elite tutors, private chefs—and yet, she lived as a phantom, excluded from the grand theatrics of the Kim dynasty's public mythology. Where other children played in parks, she walked marble halls under the gaze of bodyguards. Where others learned to make friends, she learned discretion, silence, and the art of observation.

Her father's affection for her was real, but complicated by political necessity. Kim Jong-il, a man obsessed with succession and legacy, understood that his daughter could never be an heir in the traditional sense. And yet, he saw something in her—sharpness, control, resolve. She was different from her brothers. More cunning. More adaptable. She asked questions not out of rebellion, but to understand. To know her place and how best to control it.

The death of Kim Il-sung in 1994 marked a pivotal moment. As North Korea plunged into mourning and chaos, the already-insular family turned further inward. The famine that swept through the country would kill hundreds of thousands, but inside the high-walled compounds of Pyongyang's elite, the children were protected. They watched the country bleed from a distance. And in that distance, a dangerous duality formed within Yo-jong: empathy for the people was replaced by an understanding of the machinery that caused their suffering. Her task was not to fix the machine, but to one day master it.

Even in her earliest years, Kim Yo-jong's handlers reported her emotional intelligence to be exceptional. She could read moods, anticipate desires, charm and disarm with calculated innocence. Unlike her brother Jong-un, who sometimes struggled with temper and impulsivity, Yo-jong was deliberate. She learned not to speak unless necessary. She learned to listen first, then act. And she internalized the most critical lesson of all: loyalty is survival.

Born in the shadows, she was conditioned to remain there. Her grooming did not include traditional statecraft or military drills but an immersion in secrecy and performance. Her tools would not be guns or commands, but perception, nuance, and timing. She would become the invisible hand—soft, persistent, and lethal.

Later, her emergence on the world stage would seem sudden. But for those who had studied the Kim dynasty closely, her arrival was inevitable. The girl born in silence had not only survived in the shadows—she had made them her domain. And one day, she would step from them, fully formed, cloaked not in armor but in ambiguity.

In a regime built on myth, she was the blank page. And in time, she would write her own legend—one whisper at a time.

A SWISS SECRET

Far from the rigid confines of Pyongyang, under the snow-draped peaks of the Swiss Alps, Kim Yo-jong lived an improbable chapter of her life. She and her brother, Kim Jong-un, were enrolled in a private school in Bern, Switzerland, during the mid to late 1990s. To the world, they were the children of diplomats. To their teachers and classmates, they were quiet, well-dressed, and exotic. But behind the carefully constructed facade was one of the most astonishing secrets of the Cold War's lingering aftermath: the future leaders of North Korea, walking daily among unsuspecting Westerners.

Switzerland was chosen with precision. It offered the anonymity the regime required, the neutrality needed for safe harbor, and the sophistication to expose the children to a world their parents had only spoken of in strategic whispers. Kim Yo-jong was registered under a pseudonym—just like her brother. Their guardians were intelligence handlers from Pyongyang posing as staffers at the North Korean embassy. And though they were enrolled separately, their paths often converged under the careful watch of their entourage.

For the first time in their lives, the Kim children lived outside the iron curtain of Juche ideology. They took classes with students from across the globe, learned European history, struggled with German and French, and experienced something that had no place in the Hermit Kingdom: freedom. Freedom to speak, to choose, to question. It was intoxicating—and dangerous.

Kim Yo-jong absorbed her surroundings like a sponge. She wasn't as gregarious as her brother, nor did she exhibit the same social bravado. But she was sharper. More watchful. More deliberate in her interactions. Her teachers often remarked on her poise, her grace, and her uncanny ability to blend in without ever truly revealing herself. She understood her role instinctively: to observe, not to engage; to experience, not to be changed.

Despite the rare exposure to the outside world, the children were constantly reminded of who they were. Their accommodations were separate from the rest. Their lives were regimented by the schedule of their handlers. Their food was imported when possible, and any contact with Western cultural influences was carefully screened. Still, some things slipped through. Kim Yo-jong saw how young girls in Europe carried themselves—confident, expressive, ambitious. She watched how women were treated—not as mere supporters of men, but as individuals with dreams of leadership and power. It left an impression that would later shape her strategy.

Meanwhile, the North Korean state had ensured that their presence remained undisclosed. The Swiss government, though aware, maintained plausible deniability. After all, these were the children of a nuclear-armed regime. They were not to be disturbed, and in exchange, Switzerland received a veil of silence over its own dealings. It was a diplomatic arrangement, transactional and cold—but effective.

Life in Bern offered moments of joy. The children went skiing in the Alps, ate chocolate, and on occasion, visited places like Disneyland Paris. Yet every excursion came with risk. Every smile was part of the mask. And the handlers never let them forget that their lives belonged to Pyongyang, not to the Alps.

Then, without warning, they vanished.

In the early 2000s, both Kim Jong-un and Kim Yo-jong were pulled from Switzerland. Their files were erased. Their teachers were instructed to forget. The other students barely noticed—they were just two more international kids who moved away. But in reality, the regime had decided it was time. The children had seen enough. Now, they would be returned to the shadows.

For Kim Yo-jong, Switzerland was not merely a chapter—it was a revelation. She learned the contrast between illusion and reality, between liberty and loyalty. She understood that even the most open societies could be manipulated if one knew how to play the part. And she realized that true control was not about brute force—it was about information, perception, and precision.

Bern did not westernize her. It trained her. In the art of assimilation. In the weaponization of ambiguity. In the strength of silence. The Swiss secret was not that she had lived there. The real secret was what she had learned.

And in the years to come, that knowledge would return with her—to a country that would have no idea what she had become.

THE PHANTOM SIBLINGS

In the covert world of North Korea's ruling elite, visibility is a tool of propaganda, and invisibility is a weapon of power. For Kim Yo-jong and her brother Kim Jong-un, childhood was defined not by innocence or openness, but by a strategic absence. They were phantom siblings—present in the world but erased from its record, molded in secrecy, and trained under an ideological regime that viewed transparency as treason.

Upon their return from Switzerland, the siblings were immediately submerged into the opaque and hierarchical depths of North Korean political life. Their previous lives as students in the West were buried beneath state-crafted myths, and their identities were slowly reconstructed to fit the demands of dynastic continuity. For a time, they vanished. There were no photos, no mentions in state media, no whispers in the corridors of Pyongyang's officialdom. It was as though they had never existed.

This vanishing act was by design. The Kim regime has long weaponized secrecy, using the absence of information to control narrative and perception. To know too much is to give opponents a tactical advantage. To know nothing is to foster awe, speculation, and fear. In the early 2000s, Kim Jong-il was grappling with questions of succession. His health was in quiet decline. The political elite buzzed with uncertainty. And yet, he said little. He revealed nothing. Instead, he began testing his children in silence.

Kim Yo-jong was assigned a role in the background. At first, she was not given a title, but responsibilities were quietly delegated. She was to observe the central workings of the Korean Workers' Party. She attended meetings but did not speak. She studied state broadcasts but did not appear on camera. She read internal memos, learned the codes of hierarchy, and most importantly, watched how her brother was being shaped into the next leader.

Their relationship was a complex one—equal parts sibling intimacy and political calculus. Jong-un, though younger in demeanor, was chosen to carry the family torch. He was male, strong-featured, and carried an eerie resemblance to his grandfather Kim Il-sung, the revolutionary founder of North Korea. Appearance mattered, especially in a regime that worshipped bloodlines and visual symbolism. But Yo-jong's role was no less critical. She would be the unseen hand, the backstage architect of the brother's rise, and the guardian of their collective myth.

What made them truly phantom-like was how their presence began to influence state affairs even before the public knew who they were. Internal reshuffling in the propaganda department, shifts in the tone of state messaging, subtle changes in diplomatic posturing—these were the fingerprints of a rising shadow. Foreign intelligence agencies began picking up whispers. Analysts noticed a new polish to Pyongyang's messaging, a softer veneer placed over brutal policy. Something—or someone—was directing it.

Still, neither sibling was formally introduced to the world. Jong-un was first acknowledged only after Kim Jong-il's stroke in 2008, and even then, it was in carefully managed leaks. Yo-jong remained completely hidden. Her name was not printed. Her image not broadcast. She was the phantom behind the phantom.

Their dual emergence in later years would seem sudden to the outside world. But the truth was, by the time Kim Jong-il died in 2011, both siblings had already been active participants in the regime's machinery for years. Yo-jong, in particular, had cultivated a network of loyal officials within the party's propaganda apparatus, quietly rising through its ranks. She didn't command attention; she curated it. Her approach was always surgical: influence without exposure, control without credit.

The phantom siblings became a dual force—one overt, one covert. Jong-un would become the face of the regime, with its missiles and military parades. Yo-jong would become its soul, sculpting the narrative that cloaked its violence in plausible diplomacy. Where he ruled with presence, she ruled with absence. And in North Korea, absence often speaks louder than words.

By the time her name was finally uttered on state television, Kim Yo-jong was already a master of the game. The girl who had once disappeared from a Swiss classroom had re-emerged—not as a daughter, not as a sister, but as the regime's phantom architect.

The world had been watching one Kim. It had failed to see the other.

Until now.

AUNT KO

and the Disappearing Children

In the clandestine theater of North Korea's succession saga, few figures loom as mysteriously and crucially as Ko Yong-suk, the aunt of Kim Yo-jong and Kim Jong-un. A dancer turned confidante, and eventually a fugitive, Aunt Ko's life intersected with the formative years of the Kim children in ways that would profoundly shape their future. Though her role was concealed for decades, the quiet influence she wielded during their European exile would ripple through history.

When Ko Yong-hui, the consort of Kim Jong-il and mother of Yo-jong, fell ill and her presence within the family weakened, a maternal vacuum formed in the lives of the young siblings. It was Ko Yong-suk—her sister—who was dispatched to Europe in the mid-1990s to act as guardian, caretaker, and supervisor for the children. Her assignment was unspoken but critical: shield the heirs, reinforce loyalty, and ensure they returned to North Korea prepared, obedient, and intact.

In Switzerland, Ko maintained the official story. She was a relative of diplomatic staff, managing the day-to-day lives of two children with suspiciously elite privileges and an armored cocoon of bodyguards. She arranged their schooling, oversaw their behavior, and reported their development to handlers in Pyongyang. Yet Ko was more than a minder. She became, by necessity and proximity, a surrogate mother.

Kim Yo-jong, especially, formed a quiet bond with her aunt. Ko was one of the few adults who offered her both affection and discipline. She was firm but fair, critical but protective. She read stories to her, corrected her posture, scolded her for mischief, and whispered the importance of honor and loyalty. But Ko also exposed the children—unintentionally or not—to glimpses of a different world. She admired the freedoms of the West, envied its transparency, and began to question the unrelenting demands of her brother-in-law's regime.

The children's lives were tightly managed, but their innocence created cracks in the wall of secrecy. Teachers grew curious. Local residents speculated. Questions began to rise in whispers: Why were these "diplomatic" children surrounded by security? Why did they disappear for weeks at a time? Why were they never allowed to visit others or speak of their past? But Ko kept the children in line, and the cover story held.

Then, as suddenly as they had arrived, the children were gone. Pulled back to Pyongyang without fanfare, without warning, and without goodbyes. Kim Jong-il had decided their Western education had run its course. The dynasty required heirs who understood the West—but who would never be seduced by it.

Ko Yong-suk remained behind for a time, still cloaked in diplomatic ambiguity. But by 2001, she made a fateful decision. Along with her husband

and children, Ko defected. Escaping through the U.S. Embassy in Geneva, she vanished into the American intelligence system, reappearing years later in suburban anonymity on the East Coast of the United States. Her defection was a blow to the regime—not because she held secrets (which she did), but because she had cared for the next generation.

Ko would later describe Kim Yo-jong in interviews as "sharp, proud, and very aware of who she was." Her memories of the young girl painted a picture of early ambition, emotional control, and an innate understanding of power. She saw in Yo-jong a child who did not just follow orders, but interpreted them. A child who could mimic emotion, but was never ruled by it.

The regime erased Ko's name from history. Her sister, Ko Yong-hui, was retroactively glorified as "Mother of the Nation." Ko Yong-suk was declared a traitor. Her face, once familiar in the homes of the elite, became a ghost. But within Kim Yo-jong's psyche, the presence of her aunt likely remained—a complicated blend of affection, abandonment, and betrayal.

The disappearing children had returned to North Korea, their Swiss chapter sealed. But they did not return unmarked. Aunt Ko's defection would become a silent trauma—a reminder that loyalty could fracture, that family could fail, and that even in the inner sanctum, trust was dangerous.

Years later, when Kim Yo-jong began managing state purges and internal disciplinary campaigns, some whispered that she had internalized that lesson. The closer someone stands to power, the more dangerous their potential betrayal.

And so, Aunt Ko disappeared from the world of the Kims—but not from the mind of the girl she helped raise.

RETURN TO THE MOTHERLAND

The journey from the snow-kissed serenity of Switzerland back to the rigid austerity of Pyongyang was not a return—it was a reincarnation. When Kim Yo-jong and her brother Kim Jong-un were abruptly pulled out of their private schooling in Europe in the early 2000s, they did not simply come home. They were summoned. Called back to the empire of their bloodline to be reshaped, repurposed, and silently deployed within the regime's architecture.

For Kim Yo-jong, the transition was especially stark. Gone were the Swiss gardens, the quiet libraries, the multicultural exposure. In their place rose the gray, monolithic skyline of the North Korean capital—streets lined with marching soldiers, buildings echoing with revolutionary slogans, and every public square turned into a stage of obedience. From the moment she stepped off the aircraft, Yo-jong was no longer a girl. She was a daughter of Juche.

Her arrival was not public. The people of North Korea never knew the sister of their future

Supreme Leader had been living abroad. She was inserted into elite life through a corridor of secrecy, absorbed into the ruling compound where ideology was ritual and surveillance a way of life. There, in the shadow of her father's declining health, she began the second phase of her training—not as a citizen, but as an instrument.

Kim Jong-il was not an affectionate father in public, but privately, he invested in his daughter's growth. He assigned her mentors from within the inner circle, tasked them with refining her understanding of statecraft, propaganda, and internal loyalty. She was instructed in the writings of her grandfather, Kim Il-sung, and drilled in the speeches of her father. She was taught how to interpret dissent, how to evaluate loyalty, and how to manipulate power without appearing to wield it.

She learned quickly. Faster than expected. Her Swiss exposure gave her an edge—an intuitive understanding of how the outside world perceived North Korea and how the regime could use that perception as a weapon. She observed how different power looked from the inside: not loud or blustering, but silent, sharp, and unrelenting. She absorbed the nuances of rank, the importance of deference, the codes of speech, the choreography of obedience.

Yet, despite her growing role, she remained invisible to the public. There were no announcements. No posters. She existed only in internal documents and whispered references. Within the party's Propaganda and Agitation Department, she began her ascent—not as a leader, but as a force behind leaders. She reviewed speeches. Edited broadcasts. Oversaw messaging campaigns. Slowly, subtly, she became the curator of the regime's image.

Her brother, meanwhile, was being groomed for the throne. He was placed in front of cameras, introduced in select appearances, and trained in military etiquette. But it was Yo-jong who often orchestrated these moments. She arranged the angles, selected the language, chose the tone. Even then, she understood that narrative, more than force, would define their dynasty's survival.

By 2009, insiders began to speak of her influence. She was seen walking beside her brother in party events, always one step behind, always unaddressed—but always there. Her presence was both intimate and strategic. She had access that few others enjoyed. She was his advisor, his confidante, and—some suspected—his conscience.

The return to the motherland had not broken her. It had forged her.

Pyongyang was not just her home; it was her proving ground. In the space between monuments and surveillance cameras, Kim Yo-jong became something the regime had never fully anticipated: a woman of power, born not from ambition, but from design. Her return was not the end of her education—it was its activation.

And though the people of North Korea still had no name or face to match the ghost in the palace, her shadow stretched across every newsroom, every stage-managed applause, every line of ideology. She had returned to the motherland, but not to be seen.

She had returned to control what others would see.

THE APPRENTICE OF PROPAGANDA

In the hidden corridors of North Korea's bureaucracy, where images are more powerful than missiles and words can kill faster than bullets, Kim Yo-jong found her calling. She didn't inherit an army or a ministry. She was not appointed through ceremony or announced by decree. Instead, she was entrusted with something far more potent and insidious: the truth as the regime defined it. She became the apprentice of propaganda.

Her entry into the Propaganda and Agitation Department (PAD) of the Korean Workers' Party was quiet and calculated. The PAD is no ordinary department. It is the nerve center of perception—the director of the collective imagination of the North Korean people. It oversees all media, all education, all artistic expression, and every pixel and syllable that reaches the public. It doesn't just inform; it sculpts reality. And within that machinery, Yo-jong would become both technician and visionary.

Under the shadow of her father's legacy and the watchful eyes of the party elite, she began with menial but vital tasks: reviewing speeches, coordinating newspaper headlines, and editing television scripts. But unlike her peers, Yo-jong brought with her the rarest of weapons in North Korea—outside perspective. Her time in Switzerland, her fluency in global optics, and her understanding of how foreigners perceived the regime made her invaluable. She knew that the war of the 21st century would not be fought solely with arms, but with influence.

She studied how Western governments manipulated media. She dissected American branding strategies. She analyzed how China shaped internal messaging for external audiences. She began to weave all these tactics into North Korea's messaging—subtly at first, and then boldly. Under her influence, Pyongyang's propaganda began to evolve. The tone of its state broadcasts shifted. The imagery became more polished. The messaging more sophisticated. Gone were the clunky slogans of past decades. In their place emerged a narrative of resilience, modernity, and moral superiority.

But Yo-jong wasn't merely modernizing the message—she was crafting a myth. The myth of her brother as a young, energetic, and enlightened leader; the myth of North Korea as a misunderstood nation, unfairly demonized; and the myth of progress under the careful stewardship of the ruling family. Her fingerprints were all over campaigns that depicted Kim Jong-un visiting orphanages, smiling at farmers, giving advice to scientists. She wasn't behind the camera, but she was behind the idea.

Inside party meetings, her influence grew. While her rank was not officially high, her opinion mattered. Senior propagandists and generals alike deferred to her quiet authority. She spoke rarely, but when she did, it was precise, emotionless, and final. She was meticulous in her control of every image that left Pyongyang. Every public appearance by her brother was a curated event. Every newspaper headline, a calculated move. Nothing was accidental.

Analysts abroad began to take note. Defectors spoke of a "woman in the shadows" who was redefining the face of the regime. Intelligence agencies traced the shift in propaganda style and found its epicenter: Kim Yo-jong. She had transformed from assistant to architect, from observer to operator.

What made her dangerous was not just her control over messaging—it was her vision. She didn't see propaganda as a tool for distraction, but as a mechanism of dominance. She knew that controlling what people believe is more effective than controlling what they fear. She ensured that loyalty was not just expected but internalized. Through music, art, slogans, and cinema, she rewired how North Koreans saw themselves and their place in the world.

When dissent rose, she didn't silence it with guns—she drowned it in narrative. When questions emerged, she buried them in praise. She wielded contradiction as a weapon, making her people believe in both progress and hardship, strength and suffering, peace and perpetual war. And through it all, she remained unseen by the very people she manipulated.

By the time Kim Jong-il died and her brother officially rose to power, Kim Yo-jong was no longer an apprentice. She was a master. She had not only shaped the regime's image but had fused her identity into its lifeblood. The regime didn't just speak her language—it echoed her mind.

In North Korea, where monuments rot but myths endure, she had become the keeper of illusion. The apprentice of propaganda had become its high priestess.

And the world had yet to realize that its most dangerous enemy was not the man on the podium, but the woman behind the curtain.

SISTER IN THE SHADOWS

Kim Yo-jong never needed a title to hold power. She wielded it from the shadows, camouflaged by the public spectacle of her brother's reign. As Kim Jong-un ascended to the role of Supreme Leader, the world focused on his military parades, his nuclear rhetoric, and his carefully sculpted image. Few noticed the slender figure who lingered in the background—present but peripheral, silent but significant.

Her role as "sister to the Supreme Leader" offered the perfect cover. In a regime dominated by patriarchal tradition and hierarchical protocol, she was underestimated by default. But inside the walls of Pyongyang's command structures, her influence was increasingly undeniable. She attended key strategy sessions. She reviewed the seating arrangements at diplomatic events. She ghostwrote lines for state broadcasts. And she oversaw the details of every message her brother delivered to the world.

To the inner circle, she was more than a sibling—she was a shield and a sensor. She anticipated threats before they materialized, intercepted internal gossip, and kept the machinery of image running smoothly. If Jong-un was the face of the dynasty, Yo-jong was its eyes and ears. Her silence was strategic, not submissive.

She understood the dangers of visibility. Her father had maintained control by retreating from the spotlight, letting mystery shield him from critique. She emulated that strategy. Instead of vying for open recognition, she embedded herself in the folds of governance. She became a whisper in the ears of party elites, a guiding hand on her brother's shoulder, a shadow moving quietly from one corridor to the next.

There were moments when she appeared—brief flashes of her figure during state funerals, military inspections, or ceremonial events. But her appearances were never incidental. They were calculated tests. When she stood at her brother's side at Kim Jong-il's funeral in 2011, some saw it as symbolic. Others knew it was a signal: she was more than family. She was function.

Her discretion allowed her a freedom others in the regime lacked. She could maneuver without the pressure of expectation, issue orders without being directly quoted, and gather intelligence without being seen as a threat. Ministers who underestimated her rarely did so twice. Those who challenged her found themselves reassigned, or worse—erased from the internal hierarchy altogether.

Foreign observers remained confused. Intelligence reports mentioned her in passing. Analysts speculated on her role but lacked concrete evidence. Even the most sophisticated satellites and surveillance could not penetrate the opaqueness of her movements. In an age of total visibility, Kim Yo-jong remained elusive by design.

But within North Korea, her influence became clearer. Cultural productions began to subtly reflect her tastes. The tone of children's programs shifted. The lyrics of state-approved songs changed. The way news anchors presented information bore her imprint. In all these arenas, her presence was felt, not seen. She had become the embodiment of what North Korea most prized: loyalty without arrogance, presence without provocation.

For her brother, she was indispensable. Unlike previous advisors, she did not seek power for herself—at least not openly. She protected his legacy as much as his reputation. She prepped him for speeches, coached him for summits, and even corrected his tone in private discussions. She knew his weaknesses and managed them. She understood his strengths and magnified them. Behind closed doors, their conversations were strategic—siblings bound not just by blood, but by a shared destiny.

Yet there were risks. In a regime that has devoured its own members for less, her proximity to power made her vulnerable. Her survival depended on balance: too distant, and she'd be forgotten; too bold, and she'd be feared. But Yo-jong knew this dance. She choreographed it with precision.

As North Korea marched through diplomatic upheavals and military escalations, the sister in the shadows grew stronger. She did not need statues or slogans. Her legacy was being written in decisions, in strategies, in the culture of silence she so masterfully curated.

By the time her name was formally acknowledged by the state media, it was not an introduction—it was a revelation. For years, she had already ruled from behind the veil.

And now, the veil was beginning to lift.

FIRST LADY OF FEAR

In regimes built on fear, the most terrifying figures are rarely those who scream the loudest. They are the ones who speak softly, smile politely, and disappear people with a nod. By the late 2010s, Kim Yo-jong had quietly evolved from a behind-the-scenes strategist to something far more formidable: the First Lady of Fear.

While Kim Jong-un consolidated his grip over North Korea's military and nuclear command, his sister built a parallel empire—one that governed perception, punished disloyalty, and sculpted the face of tyranny into something deceptively elegant. Her ascent was not a coronation. It was a campaign of erasure and construction: eliminating rivals, suppressing dissent, and weaving a new mythology around the regime.

At first, her authority was assumed to be limited to propaganda. But this illusion began to crack with a series of inexplicable purges inside the party ranks. Officials who had decades of loyalty suddenly vanished. Generals were demoted without explanation. Artists and broadcasters disappeared from the airwaves. And with each silence, a name whispered from the shadows: Kim Yo-jong.

Insiders revealed that she had taken direct control over the Propaganda and Agitation Department, wielding its power with unprecedented autonomy. She reviewed not just speeches, but surveillance reports. She didn't merely approve scripts—she decided which voices would be allowed to speak at all. Her influence extended to the Ministry of State Security, where political loyalty was monitored with surgical precision.

One of the most chilling indicators of her influence came in 2016, when a group of senior cultural officials were reportedly executed after a failed media campaign. The reason? It failed to evoke the emotional tone she had prescribed. This wasn't censorship. This was autocratic art direction—with a body count.

Behind the polished portraits of the Kim dynasty, Yo-jong ran a system of performance terror. Loyalty was no longer measured by ideology, but by exact mimicry of her vision. Disobedience, even in tone or phrasing, was interpreted as rebellion. To cross her aesthetic line was to court disappearance.

She began issuing internal directives through coded language. Her words—precise, cold, bureaucratic—became synonymous with finality. Unlike her brother, whose wrath was often performative and impulsive, hers was deliberate and unflinching. She did not yell. She did not curse. She signed a paper—and someone ceased to exist.

Defectors who had once worked in the state apparatus described her presence in meetings as unnerving. "She doesn't speak much," one recalled, "but when she does, everyone stops breathing." Her authority was unspoken, but absolute. She could rewrite entire programs with a single remark. Her critiques were few but devastating. And in a system built on paranoia, ambiguity was her deadliest weapon.

The fear she inspired was not only internal. Beyond the DMZ, South Korean officials began to track her rhetoric closely. When she released a statement, it carried a different weight. More venomous, more personal, more final. Her insults were not diplomatic jabs—they were declarations. When she called defectors "human scum," it wasn't hyperbole. It was a warning.

Western intelligence began to reassess her status. Analysts who had once dismissed her as a "communications figure" now realized she was at the center of the regime's decision-making. She was not a messenger—she was a messenger with the authority to kill.

And yet, paradoxically, she maintained the image of civility. In photos, she appeared refined, modestly dressed, smiling with the grace of a stateswoman. Her posture was disarming. Her mannerisms serene. This juxtaposition made her more dangerous. She was the embodiment of duality: charm layered over coercion, diplomacy as a disguise for domination.

Her power culminated in key summits where she accompanied her brother to meetings with foreign leaders. She whispered in his ear. She monitored every camera angle. She analyzed every handshake. And behind the smiles exchanged between heads of state, she watched for weakness—ready to turn it into strategy.

Internally, her myth deepened. To party officials, she was omniscient. To generals, she was untouchable. And to the people—though most did not know her name—she was a presence in every broadcast, every chant, every silence. The First Lady of Fear did not need a crown or a uniform. Her rule was unmarked by ceremony but unmistakable in consequence.

She had mastered a darker kind of leadership—one that required no spotlight, no cheers, and no throne. Only obedience.

And in North Korea, fear is the most obedient servant of all.

DIPLOMATIC ILLUSION

In February 2018, as athletes from around the world descended upon Pyeongchang for the Winter Olympics, South Korea found itself hosting an unlikely and unprecedented guest. She entered the stadium with the grace of a seasoned diplomat, seated just meters away from the Vice President of the United States. Her composure was immaculate, her smile understated, her demeanor calm. For a fleeting moment, the world glimpsed what appeared to be a softer face of North Korea. Her name was Kim Yo-jong.

The illusion had begun.

Kim Yo-jong's appearance at the Olympics was the most significant diplomatic moment for North Korea in decades. No member of the ruling Kim family had ever set foot in South Korea since the armistice of 1953. Her presence was not just symbolic—it was historic. Dressed modestly in black and accompanied by a carefully curated delegation, she brought with her an invitation to dialogue, a message of peace, and an expertly orchestrated performance.

Observers were stunned. Western media hailed her as "North Korea's Ivanka Trump," captivated by her poise and political bearing. Journalists speculated on a possible thaw between the Koreas. Camera flashes captured her every movement, and her name trended across international platforms. But the real brilliance of the moment lay in its choreography. Every step, every smile, every silent nod had been calculated months in advance.

Behind the diplomatic mask was a woman who had been scripting the regime's narrative for years. This was not a debut—it was a reveal. Kim Yo-jong's role in the Olympics was the culmination of a long campaign to soften North Korea's image and reposition her brother's regime as capable of negotiation, modernization, and even peace. It was, of course, a lie. But it was a beautiful one.

During the opening ceremony, she sat calmly as the world watched her watching. She extended a handwritten letter from Kim Jong-un to South Korean President Moon Jae-in, inviting him to Pyongyang. The gesture, delivered with quiet elegance, was enough to send diplomatic shockwaves through the region. The North Korean regime, once isolated and untouchable, was suddenly a participant in the global order. And at the center of it all was Yo-jong.

Her command of symbolism was unmatched. The decision to attend the Olympics, the carefully chosen attire, the selective press interactions—it was all a symphony of statecraft. While others saw a softening, Yo-jong was consolidating control. She had managed to recast the North Korean leadership in a new light, even as the gulags remained full and missile tests continued in secret.

South Korean officials were not naïve. They recognized the propaganda embedded in her charm. But they also knew the power of perception. Engaging her, even if symbolic, offered a potential path to dialogue. The illusion of peace, in diplomacy, can be as potent as peace itself.

Yo-jong's visit did more than charm the international community—it reframed North Korea's position in regional geopolitics. In the months that followed, her brother met with world leaders, including Chinese President Xi Jinping and U.S. President Donald Trump. But many of the logistics, preparations, and image management behind these meetings were guided by her hand. She was not just shaping her country's foreign policy narrative; she was performing it.

Her presence at these high-stakes events was subtle but strategic. She hovered at the edges of press conferences, stood behind her brother during handshakes, and disappeared before the photo ops ended. She wasn't the main act—she was the director.

The illusion began to fade as talks stalled and provocations resumed. But by then, the world had already recalibrated its image of the North Korean regime. The memory of Kim Yo-jong at the Olympics lingered. The idea that North Korea could be diplomatic, even charming, had been planted. And in the theater of international politics, impressions last longer than facts.

Kim Yo-jong's diplomatic debut was not about peace. It was about power. She had rebranded a dictatorship, if only temporarily. She had performed humility, grace, and openness. But behind the curtain, she remained what she always had been: a sentinel of tyranny, cloaked in elegance.

It was not diplomacy. It was illusion. And for a moment, it worked.

THE OLYMPIC DEBUT

February 9, 2018. The opening ceremony of the Winter Olympics in Pyeongchang was a spectacle of light, performance, and geopolitical theater. But no moment captured the world's imagination more than the silent entrance of a woman who had never before stepped into the global spotlight. Kim Yo-jong, sister of North Korea's Supreme Leader, descended into South Korea not with an army, but with a smile and a letter. Her mere presence rewrote decades of hostility—and for a brief moment, the peninsula held its breath.

The moment was more than symbolic. It was revolutionary.

No member of the Kim dynasty had ever crossed the heavily fortified border to the South. Kim Yo-jong's appearance was not just unexpected—it was unprecedented. Flanked by bodyguards and South Korean hosts, she moved with quiet confidence, her composure unshaken by the weight of history. She did not speak often, but when she did, her words were diplomatic, measured, and sharply effective.

The international press erupted in fascination. She was called the "Ivanka Trump of North Korea," a label that both trivialized and revealed the West's astonishment that such poise and political weight could emanate from Pyongyang. Headlines obsessed over her expressions, her clothing, her posture. But behind the superficial analysis, something far more significant was unfolding.

Kim Yo-jong was executing the most dangerous charm offensive in the history of modern autocracies.

She carried with her a message from Kim Jong-un—an invitation to South Korea's President Moon Jae-in to visit Pyongyang. This letter, delivered with grace and modesty, was no mere gesture of goodwill. It was a strategic chess move designed to shift regional power dynamics, weaken U.S. leverage, and sow division among allies. And it worked. The invitation dominated news cycles, reframing North Korea's image from rogue pariah to misunderstood participant in global diplomacy.

Throughout the games, Yo-jong was omnipresent yet distant. She clapped politely during ceremonies, smiled gently at athletes, and engaged in symbolic gestures of reconciliation. One particularly dramatic image showed her seated behind U.S. Vice President Mike Pence, who conspicuously avoided acknowledging her. The photo, widely circulated, became emblematic of the new complexity of Korean diplomacy—where the most potent force was not a general or a missile, but a woman who had never before been seen in public.

But this was no debutante's performance. This was a carefully calibrated operation. Every appearance, every word, and every silence had been rehearsed. North Korean state media back home framed her trip as a gesture of peace and power. Her manner—quiet, respectful, deferential—masked the strategy unfolding beneath the surface.

Behind closed doors, she was less demure. In meetings with South Korean officials, she was assertive, confident, and at times, sharply direct. She spoke of cooperation but insisted on equal footing. She rejected pity and emphasized pride. She was not there to apologize—she was there to negotiate from a position of calculated strength.

For Kim Yo-jong, the Olympic debut was a test of influence. Could she, a woman from a regime known for brutality and isolation, transform the narrative with a few days of pageantry? Could she redirect global discourse through posture alone? The answer, in many ways, was yes. The media coverage, the diplomatic engagement, and the cautious optimism that followed all validated the potency of her performance.

But the performance came with a cost. Critics pointed out that her charm masked a regime that continued to starve its people and execute its enemies. Human rights activists condemned the uncritical coverage she received. Others warned that she was not a new leader—but the guardian of an old order, simply repackaged for modern eyes.

Still, within North Korea, her mission was hailed as a triumph. Upon her return, she was celebrated internally and rewarded with greater authority. Her success at Pyeongchang solidified her role not just as a senior propagandist, but as a principal envoy of the regime's international ambitions. She had proven herself not only to her brother, but to the elite circles of power that governed the world's most secretive state.

The Olympic debut was more than an event—it was a blueprint. A demonstration that in the age of global optics, image could be more persuasive than ideology. That a woman, silent for most of her life, could become the face of North Korea's new mask.

And in the games of diplomacy, Kim Yo-jong had won the opening round.

THE ARCHITECT OF SOFT POWER

Power in the 21st century is no longer confined to tanks, treaties, or tyrants who roar from podiums. In the shadows of global diplomacy, influence is crafted with precision, whispered into microphones, and cloaked in the language of hope. Kim Yo-jong understood this before most world leaders did. She wasn't just an emissary of her brother's regime—she was the architect of its soft power.

In the wake of her Olympic appearance, Yo-jong's portfolio quietly expanded. She was no longer confined to propaganda and image management within North Korea; now, she was shaping how the world saw—and reacted to—the regime itself. Her approach was calculated: maintain the machinery of repression at home, while crafting a seductive mirage of reform and diplomacy abroad.

Soft power, as coined by political scientist Joseph Nye, refers to a country's ability to shape preferences and influence others through attraction rather than coercion. For most of its history, North Korea had none. It was a pariah, reviled, mocked, feared. But under Yo-jong's influence, it began to rebrand—not as a threat, but as a misunderstood nation seeking peace, security, and respect.

She understood the mechanics of global media. She knew that carefully curated moments—handshakes, letters, photo ops—could do more to shift public opinion than military declarations. So she orchestrated them. She ensured that the regime's diplomatic gestures were accompanied by symbols of unity: inter-Korean meetings with shared meals, performances by North Korean artists, footage of soldiers smiling instead of marching.

But beneath the surface, she never loosened control. The prison camps remained full. The surveillance state grew more sophisticated. Defectors were hunted with increasing aggression. And yet, Yo-jong succeeded in crafting a narrative that captivated audiences beyond the 38th parallel. She made it possible for people to speak of Kim Jong-un not as a tyrant, but as a potential peacemaker. And she did so without ever uttering more than a few words in public.

Her genius lay in contrast. She placed moments of apparent warmth against a backdrop of hostility, and the world was so hungry for peace that it ignored the backdrop. When her brother held summits with President Moon or President Trump, it was Yo-jong who ensured that the lighting was right, the messaging tight, and the visuals globally digestible. When delegations from Pyongyang met with international counterparts, it was her influence that softened the tone, adjusted the gestures, and managed the optics.

She made North Korea's diplomatic face not just tolerable—but strangely compelling.

Behind closed doors, she continued to wield iron-fisted authority. She was reported to have personally signed off on the punishment of officials who failed to meet her communications standards. She restructured the propaganda apparatus, emphasizing film, online content, and visual storytelling over dry ideological speeches. She approved short documentaries showing Pyongyang's skyline, its pristine metro stations, and its "happy citizens"—all pieces of curated fiction aimed at reshaping international perception.

Analysts from the West began to view her as the most sophisticated strategist North Korea had ever produced. She had combined the aesthetic restraint of Cold War-era Soviet diplomacy with the media-savviness of Silicon Valley. She wasn't selling freedom—she was selling familiarity. And in doing so, she disarmed critics and confused opponents.

Yet, it was all built on a lie.

The soft power she constructed was a theatrical set—convincing, but hollow. North Korea had not changed. It had only changed costume. And like any architect of illusion, Yo-jong understood the risks. Illusions require constant maintenance. Every misstep, every defector's testimony, every satellite image of a prison camp threatened to undo the performance. But she managed it with relentless precision.

In her hands, soft power became a weapon. Not to charm, but to disorient. Not to integrate, but to isolate on North Korea's terms. She knew that engagement on her stage meant the world had to play by her script. And she was always rewriting it.

Kim Yo-jong didn't want her country to be loved. She wanted it to be respected, feared, and misunderstood just enough to stay untouchable.

In the theater of international relations, she had built a masterpiece.

And behind every curtain, every spotlight, every carefully arranged summit table—stood the architect.

THE MEDIA STRATEGIST

In a nation where the press serves not the people but the state, control over media is not simply an asset—it is an instrument of survival. Kim Yo-jong, already embedded deep within the propaganda matrix, elevated her role from architect of message to master of strategy. She did not merely refine North Korean media—she revolutionized its purpose. She became the strategist behind every image, every phrase, every illusion.

North Korean propaganda had long relied on outdated tools: statues, slogans, grainy footage of parades. It was repetitive, rigid, and increasingly ineffective in an era of rapid global communication. Yo-jong understood this. She knew that if North Korea's narrative was to compete in the modern information war, it had to evolve. It had to speak the language of virality, visual sophistication, and emotional manipulation.

She began with television. North Korean state broadcasts were redesigned—crisper visuals, more dynamic editing, brighter colors. News anchors adopted a softer tone. Documentaries became more cinematic. Music was modernized, drawing from South Korean styles while maintaining ideological purity. She understood the psychology of rhythm and repetition. She understood the power of framing.

Yo-jong introduced a key innovation: the humanization of the Supreme Leader. Instead of only showing Kim Jong-un in military garb surveying weapons, he was increasingly shown smiling at children, touring schools, laughing with farmers. This was not accidental. It was part of a deliberate pivot to make the leadership appear more accessible—an attempt to blur the line between divinity and relatability.

She also expanded into digital media. Despite North Korea's tightly restricted internet, state-run content began appearing on platforms like YouTube and Twitter through proxy accounts managed by overseas operatives. These videos—often bizarre, sometimes compelling—portrayed life in Pyongyang as vibrant and joyful. They showed model citizens cooking meals, playing instruments, or praising the regime with wide, suspiciously rehearsed smiles.

Western analysts initially dismissed these as absurd relics of Cold War absurdity. But slowly, views climbed. Some videos were picked up by Western media outlets. Others became the subject of online speculation, parodies, and reaction videos. Even mockery served a purpose: it brought attention. And attention was the first step toward legitimacy.

Internally, Yo-jong enforced stricter discipline than ever before. State journalists were monitored closely, their scripts cross-checked by her team. Any deviation from tone or phrase could result in re-education—or worse. Reporters operated with the knowledge that a single misstep could be fatal. She installed a culture of creative rigidity—encouraging innovation, but only within the invisible walls she built.

In time, the international press began to notice a pattern. Every foreign journalist granted rare access to North Korea saw the same curated scenes. The same markets. The same cheerful citizens. All paths led to a narrative Yo-jong had crafted—a story of cautious progress, benevolent leadership, and cultural pride.

Yet her true brilliance lay in dual messaging.

While outwardly presenting a softer, more modern face to the world, internally she doubled down on ideological intensity. Educational content for children became more nationalistic. Films celebrated martyrdom and loyalty. Artworks depicted American soldiers as grotesque caricatures. She ensured that North Koreans never forgot who the enemy was—even as she courted that enemy's attention abroad.

Kim Yo-jong's media strategy turned North Korea from a caricature into a character—more complex, more enigmatic, and thus harder to confront. She created enough ambiguity to confuse global audiences. And in confusion, there is hesitation. And in hesitation, the regime survives.

She did not aim to tell the truth. She aimed to control what could be believed.

And in that game, she played the world like a seasoned strategist with a captive audience.

THE SOFT EDGE OF A HARD REGIME

Beneath the rigid militarism and doctrinaire slogans of the North Korean regime, a new strategy quietly unfolded—one that substituted steel for silk, threats for gestures, and monolithic masculinity for a new kind of female finesse. Kim Yo-jong didn't seek to soften the regime's core, but to coat its exterior with enough charm and ambiguity to delay confrontation. She became the soft edge of a hard regime.

To those within the inner sanctum of the Workers' Party, this shift was not cosmetic. It was structural. Yo-jong's influence began reshaping how the regime projected itself, not just abroad but internally. Public campaigns increasingly emphasized civic pride over blind fear. National holidays began incorporating performances and art exhibitions that mimicked global trends. Female presenters on state TV adopted more modern attire. This evolution was subtle, careful not to challenge patriarchal norms or the dynasty's supremacy—but it was undeniable.

The strategy was not to change the regime. It was to make it appear changed.

Yo-jong's genius lay in knowing that the West no longer feared North Korea's weapons—they expected them. What unnerved the West more was unpredictability, ambiguity, and moments of seeming empathy. A regime that smiled could no longer be easily bombed. A dictatorship with a "human face" could not be easily sanctioned. She weaponized these paradoxes.

Inside the regime, she promoted cultural campaigns that emphasized North Korea's uniqueness rather than its hostility. Documentaries celebrated science, sports, and agriculture. Art competitions encouraged schoolchildren to depict a hopeful, futuristic DPRK. This did not replace indoctrination—it repackaged it. Citizens still revered the leadership as gods, but now their worship was wrapped in warmth.

One of Yo-jong's key innovations was the creation of cultural diplomacy. She sent artists, musicians, and dancers abroad to perform in friendly nations. She arranged cultural exchanges that appeared innocuous but served dual purposes: to gather intelligence and to subtly introduce North Korea as a "normal" state. She curated national identity as if managing a brand.

This branding extended to humanitarian optics. When North Korea sent aid to countries hit by disaster—or hosted foreign visitors for medical or agricultural demonstrations—Yo-jong ensured the events were filmed, edited, and distributed globally. She was crafting a regime that could no longer be easily demonized. She understood the world judged by contrast, and so she created the contrast.

And yet, while the regime's exterior softened, its core grew even more brutal. Executions continued. Censorship tightened. Political prison camps expanded. Loyalty checks intensified. Dissenters vanished. Yo-jong was not liberalizing the state—she was hiding its teeth behind a velvet curtain.

Her efforts confused allies and enemies alike. Diplomats struggled to decipher if North Korea was truly shifting or simply pretending. Journalists argued over whether the changes signaled reform or manipulation. Meanwhile, the regime bought time. Time to strengthen its arsenal, to build alliances, to secure internal power.

Kim Yo-jong had transformed perception into policy. She convinced the world to look not at what North Korea was—but at what it could be.

And in that narrow window of hopeful illusion, she held open the door for a regime that remained, at its heart, as hard as ever.

THE NUCLEAR SMILE

There is a photograph that once made global headlines: Kim Jong-un, standing beside a gleaming intercontinental ballistic missile, grinning as if he were unveiling a new sports car. But just a few feet behind him, barely visible, stood Kim Yo-jong, her expression unreadable. That image captured the essence of her most dangerous paradox: a regime smiling through its nuclear menace. A nuclear smile.

While her brother held the button, it was Yo-jong who shaped the narrative around it. She understood better than anyone that raw aggression had diminishing returns. Each missile test brought condemnation, yes—but also predictability. The world knew what to expect. What they didn't expect was charm, wit, and calculated satire coming from Pyongyang's inner circle.

Yo-jong began releasing statements in her own name—sharp, sarcastic, and fiercely political. She mocked South Korean leaders. She derided the U.S. as hypocritical. She threatened retaliation not with tanks, but with metaphors. These communiqués, often released through state media or as official party comments, became events in themselves. Her voice was a new kind of weapon—less explosive, more insidious.

She crafted a unique diplomatic persona: the anti-diplomat. A woman who could flirt with the language of peace one day, and threaten annihilation the next—all while maintaining a polished public image. When her brother met with Donald Trump in Singapore and Hanoi, it was Yo-jong who ensured the visual messaging reinforced parity. No longer was North Korea the desperate petitioner—it was the bold challenger.

Nuclear diplomacy had entered the era of theater.

And Kim Yo-jong was its director.

Behind the scenes, she was involved in scripting how nuclear developments were presented to the public. Footage of missile launches was no longer grainy and erratic—it was cinematic. She insisted on multi-angle shots, slow-motion replays, and dramatic soundtracks. North Korea's nuclear program was not just a security doctrine—it was a spectacle.

But her greatest manipulation lay in how she framed the weapons not as threats, but as shields. In her messaging, nuclear arms were a response, not a provocation. A defense against U.S. hostility, a guarantee of peace, a rational safeguard. She transformed North Korea's most feared asset into its most justified necessity.

This framing extended into education and culture. School textbooks included her language. Propaganda posters featured her slogans. Even children's animations depicted missiles as protectors, not destroyers. She blurred the line between survival and provocation so effectively that many North Koreans came to believe they lived in peace—only because their country could end the world.

The smile became central. Yo-jong rebranded the nuclear posture into one of dignified deterrence. Her brother's laughter after successful launches was no longer madness—it was pride. Her own calm demeanor in threatening statements created a chilling dissonance: apocalypse, delivered with grace.

To the West, this was both confusing and disarming. How could a regime so brutal, so regressive, produce such articulate manipulation? The answer was Kim Yo-jong. She was the smile behind the arsenal. The mind behind the spectacle. The diplomat who never believed in diplomacy, but perfected its illusion.

Her nuclear smile was not a contradiction.

It was a strategy.

And it was working.

BALLOONS OVER THE DMZ

They floated like children's toys at first—harmless, even whimsical. Balloons carried by wind over the most heavily militarized border in the world. But attached to their strings were messages of war: leaflets, propaganda, USB sticks, and defiance. In return, came a storm of fury, not from Kim Jong-un, but from his sister. Kim Yo-jong had found a new theater for confrontation: the sky above the Demilitarized Zone.

For decades, defectors and South Korean activists had launched balloon campaigns over the border, sending materials into North Korea that exposed its people to banned information. These airborne acts of rebellion were often small-scale but symbolically potent. And in 2020, they drew the wrath of Kim Yo-jong in a way that few could have anticipated.

Her response was immediate and devastating.

In an official statement, she threatened to sever all communication lines with South Korea. Within days, the North destroyed the inter-Korean liaison office in Kaesong—an unprecedented act of sabotage, captured on video and broadcast around the world. The explosion wasn't just physical—it was psychological. It signaled a shift in tone, a tightening of control, and a declaration that the North's olive branches had thorns.

But what fascinated observers was not the escalation itself—it was the manner in which Yo-jong escalated it.

Her rhetoric in the official statements was personal, emotive, and unusually aggressive. She called the defectors "filthy scum" and warned the South that "by exercising my power authorized by the Supreme Leader, I gave an instruction to the departments concerned to decisively carry out the next action." It was the first time she publicly invoked her authority, independent of her brother.

This was not just a protest against leaflets—it was a power move.

Through the balloon crisis, Yo-jong made several things clear: she was no longer merely a messenger. She had operational power. She could initiate responses. She could shape policy. And perhaps most importantly, she was willing to act.

The destruction of the liaison office was a symbolic rupture of the illusion of progress. For months, North and South Korea had cultivated a delicate line of communication. It had been touted as a path to lasting dialogue. With one act, Yo-jong obliterated it. She didn't just close a door—she blew it off its hinges.

The choice of target was equally telling. The liaison office represented a shared space, a neutral zone for cautious cooperation. By destroying it, she wasn't just retaliating against activists—she was declaring an end to ambiguity. There would be no middle ground. You were either with the North, or against it.

Her role in the incident marked a dramatic public ascent. Intelligence analysts worldwide began reassessing her status. No longer a shadow operative, she was now executing decisions with material consequences. The destruction of Kaesong was her calling card.

Internally, her actions reinforced her authority. The military applauded her decisiveness. The party praised her loyalty. The people were reminded that power in the Kim dynasty no longer resided in a single figure—but in a bloodline willing to act as one.

And the balloons kept flying. Not just from the South, but from the North—this time, laced with garbage, cigarette butts, and feces. A mirror response. A grotesque parody. A statement that absurdity could be weaponized.

Kim Yo-jong had taken a symbolic conflict and turned it into a strategic play. The skies over the DMZ became her latest battlefield—not for air superiority, but for narrative control.

And she won.

THE BAD COP GETS WORSE

For years, Kim Yo-jong played the role of controlled contrast. While her brother issued explosive threats, she offered veiled warnings. While generals flexed their uniforms on camera, she sat in quiet diplomacy. But by 2022, that balance shifted. The bad cop of North Korean politics had not only emerged—it had gotten worse.

Gone were the days of polite diplomacy and ambiguous phrasing. In their place, Kim Yo-jong adopted a voice of scorn. Her public statements became laced with venom, sarcasm, and a theatrical disdain that transcended ideology. She mocked leaders, ridiculed international norms, and dismissed negotiations as the games of children. The transformation was complete. She was no longer the quiet strategist—she was the regime's voice of wrath.

In one particularly fiery address, she warned South Korea that it would face "a sea of fire" if it continued military drills with the United States. Another time, she called defectors "dogs barking at a passing caravan." Her rhetoric was designed not merely to threaten, but to humiliate.

Her shift in tone mirrored the evolution of North Korea's diplomatic posture. After the collapse of nuclear talks with the U.S., the regime recalibrated. It no longer needed to charm—it needed to confront. And Yo-jong, now seasoned and unsparing, became its lead antagonist.

She took aim at President Moon Jae-in with particular fury. Once seen as a hopeful bridge between North and South, Moon became the target of her most scathing criticisms. When Moon expressed concern about North Korean missile tests, Yo-jong fired back with insults. She dismissed his speeches as "nonsense" and called him "a man without shame."

What shocked observers was not just her tone—but her latitude. No other official in North Korea, aside from Kim Jong-un himself, could speak with such vitriol. That she did so publicly revealed her elevated status. She was not acting without permission. She was setting policy through language.

International analysts debated whether her statements were pure bluster or genuine indicators of military strategy. Some believed she was simply a tool to maintain plausible deniability—her threats could be walked back without implicating the Supreme Leader. Others saw her as an enforcer in her own right, whose words preceded real consequences.

Inside the regime, her persona took on mythical proportions. Party members whispered her name with both reverence and fear. She was respected for her discipline, feared for her precision, and admired for her ability to strike without hesitation. If her brother was the sword, she was the dagger.

What emerged was a dual image. To some in the West, she remained a mysterious figure—educated abroad, poised, and articulate. But to others, she had become something more chilling: the embodiment of ideological fury wrapped in civility.

The transformation of Kim Yo-jong from soft diplomat to venomous enforcer was no accident. It was strategy. North Korea had learned that predictable threats could be countered. But threats that came from a soft-spoken, camera-ready woman? They confused, destabilized, and provoked deeper anxiety.

By getting worse, she had become more effective.

And in the theater of confrontation, she now owned the spotlight.

OF PUPPETS AND STRINGS

Power in North Korea is a performance—and no one understood the choreography better than Kim Yo-jong. As her brother commanded attention on the world stage, it was she who pulled the strings behind the curtain. Diplomats, military figures, ministers of information—these were not autonomous leaders. They were puppets in a grand theater, their strings subtly manipulated by the only woman truly trusted in the regime's inner sanctum.

From her early days in the Propaganda and Agitation Department, Yo-jong mastered the mechanics of control. She learned that influence did not require volume—it required access, timing, and precision. She infiltrated systems not as a disruptor, but as a coordinator. She made herself indispensable. Her brother came to rely on her not for emotional support, but for operational clarity.

She ensured loyalty through a mixture of grace and terror. Officials who aligned with her were elevated. Those who questioned her, even privately, vanished. She monitored communications, read transcripts, and understood who said what to whom. In a regime where surveillance is as constant as air, she breathed it with ease.

While Kim Jong-un was the state's deity, Yo-jong was its architect of movement. She decided how policies were messaged, how meetings were staged, and how state priorities were filtered through ideology. Ministers carried her revisions into speeches. Generals adjusted their briefings after her reviews. Even top diplomats took notes from her before flying abroad.

Yet she remained unofficial. Unsworn. Unranked for much of her early influence. That made her more dangerous. She was not bound by the bureaucratic ladder. She answered only to her brother. And increasingly, he answered to her.

Foreign powers attempted to identify her proxies—men and women she placed in ministries to ensure alignment. But these operatives were rarely visible. They acted as couriers, informants, editors. Yo-jong did not need a department to rule. She needed a network. And she built one, loyal not to the state, but to her.

In this world of control, her manipulation extended even to her brother. While Kim Jong-un made headlines, Yo-jong managed his myth. She advised him on posture, tone, and narrative. She shaped how he was viewed not only externally, but internally—by the people and by the elite. When needed, she softened him. When needed, she sharpened him.

Some speculated that she had become his conscience. Others believed she was his governor, ensuring his whims did not deviate from state survival. Either way, she held immense influence over the most powerful man in the country.

The irony of the Kim dynasty is that while its power appears absolute, it is internally fragile. Factions fester, alliances shift, and paranoia reigns. In this landscape, Kim Yo-jong's mastery of strings ensured stability—because she could see the whole stage.

The puppets danced.

And no one dared to look up at the woman holding the strings.

PUTIN'S PACT

In June 2024, the world watched with stunned disbelief as two of its most controversial leaders stood side by side in Moscow: Kim Jong-un and Vladimir Putin. Their handshake wasn't just symbolic—it was strategic, signaling a recalibration of alliances that echoed Cold War geometry. But in the shadows of that summit, arranging the choreography, influencing the language, and managing the image, was Kim Yo-jong. The pact may have had her brother's signature, but its subtext bore her fingerprints.

North Korea's pivot toward Russia was not sudden. It was the culmination of years of silent coordination, economic necessity, and ideological compatibility. With China growing more cautious and the West tightening sanctions, Pyongyang found in Moscow not just a geopolitical partner, but a kindred spirit: isolated, defiant, and nuclear.

Yo-jong had long advocated for diversified alliances. Her diplomatic assessments, often disseminated through backchannel briefings, indicated that Russia's aggression in Ukraine had opened a unique window. While much of the world condemned Putin, North Korea saw opportunity. The pariah nations could form a united front—exchanging resources, intelligence, and, above all, validation.

The pact itself was military in tone but strategic in intent. It involved not just defense cooperation, but technology sharing, food aid, and joint ventures designed to bypass Western monitoring. While Kim Jong-un smiled for cameras beside Putin, it was Yo-jong who ensured that the optics conveyed parity—not desperation.

State media in Pyongyang celebrated the alliance with fanfare. Speeches were drafted, ceremonies filmed. Russian officials were shown clapping for North Korean military bands. Behind the scenes, Yo-jong managed translation teams, edited broadcasts, and directed her propaganda wing to emphasize fraternity over fear. This was not just a diplomatic event—it was a narrative milestone.

But the deeper implications of the pact were darker. Intelligence reports indicated that North Korean artillery had been routed to assist Russian operations in Ukraine. In return, Russia provided satellite data and technological assistance—advancements North Korea had long sought to improve its missile accuracy.

Yo-jong's strategy was risky but precise. She was redefining North Korea's international identity—not as a rogue, but as a stakeholder in the global conflict. She was inserting her nation into a narrative that demanded attention. And by doing so, she was forcing adversaries to recalculate their approach.

Her involvement extended beyond messaging. Reports from defectors and intercepted communications suggested she had personally coordinated logistics, oversaw bilateral discussions, and even drafted contingency language in case the summit received backlash. She wasn't a background figure—she was a tactician.

The Western response was swift but divided. Sanctions tightened. Statements were released. But Yo-jong had achieved her goal. She had moved North Korea from isolation into alliance. She had reminded the world that pariahs, too, could make pacts. And that fear, when shared, becomes strength.

Putin's pact was a diplomatic spectacle.

But for Kim Yo-jong, it was another chapter in the long game of survival.

SHADOWS OF SUCCESSION

In a regime where lineage is destiny, succession is not a matter of merit, but of myth. The death of a Supreme Leader in North Korea does not merely leave a vacancy—it threatens to unmake the very reality on which the state is built. And in the years following Kim Jong-un's consolidation of power, whispers of succession began to stir again—not because his rule faltered, but because his health did.

Kim Yo-jong was no longer just the strategist or the enforcer. She had become, in the eyes of many, the contingency plan. The shadow heir.

The rumors began to intensify in 2020, when Kim Jong-un disappeared from public view for several weeks. Analysts speculated about illness, even death. Some believed he was incapacitated. Others thought it was a political stunt. But in that void, only one figure emerged to reassure, to threaten, to lead: Kim Yo-jong.

She issued official statements in her own name, gave directives to party officials, and was seen inspecting facilities alongside military officers. For the first time, state media framed her actions not as supportive, but directive. She wasn't acting on behalf of her brother—she was acting.

Within the regime, this movement sparked anxiety. The North Korean leadership had never considered a woman as a potential head of state. The party elite, steeped in patriarchal tradition, struggled to reconcile Yo-jong's rising power with their ideological training. But they also understood her authority wasn't rooted in gender—it was rooted in proximity. She knew the codes, the players, the system. She had managed the myth of power so long that she had become indistinguishable from it.

Succession plans in North Korea are not written down. They are signaled, hinted at, and finally revealed in moments of crisis. Yo-jong's presence in those moments—firm, visible, and commanding—was itself a signal.

To the outside world, this possibility was unsettling. A regime led by a nuclear-armed woman who had orchestrated purges, manipulated image warfare, and formed strategic alliances was not necessarily more stable—it was more unpredictable.

But to some North Koreans, especially younger elites, the idea of Kim Yo-jong as a successor was not unthinkable. She represented continuity, intellect, and a level of control that no one else had displayed. She was feared, but respected. Her rise would not be smooth, but it could be inevitable.

Still, shadows cling to the idea of her leadership. The patriarchal fabric of North Korea's institutions cannot be erased with ceremony. Her claim to power would require not just bloodline, but bloodletting—a clearing of rivals, a realignment of loyalties, and an orchestration of public reverence that would surpass anything staged before.

She would not be her brother. She would not be her father. She would be something else entirely: a leader born in silence, trained in darkness, and hardened by narrative warfare.

Succession in North Korea is never certain until it is complete.

But in the shadows, her silhouette had already begun to take shape.

THE CROWNLESS QUEEN

She has no crown, no throne, and no formal title that signals her supremacy. Yet within the corridors of North Korea's absolute power, Kim Yo-jong moves with the assurance of a monarch. To some, she is the guardian of the regime. To others, she is its future. But one thing has become increasingly clear—she governs as the crownless queen.

Her ascent defies every tradition. In a dynastic state that idolizes male succession and revolutionary masculinity, she is an anomaly. Not through rebellion, but through mastery. She never asked for power. She shaped it, absorbed it, and eventually, personified it.

In official photos, she is often slightly off-center, a step behind, a glance to the side. But her eyes never wander. She watches everything. She has become the quiet center of gravity, the axis around which decisions turn. Her presence reassures insiders and warns outsiders. She does not need the language of authority—she is its tone.

This status was solidified during international crises. When her brother was absent, it was Yo-jong who delivered statements, managed optics, and directed response mechanisms. When she appeared at summits, her composure rivaled diplomats twice her age. She had studied power all her life—not in theory, but in execution.

She rewrote the expectations of leadership within the regime. No lavish displays. No cult of personality. No mass parades in her honor—yet. Her power is subtler, and because of that, more terrifying. She doesn't inspire loyalty through worship. She commands it through precision.

Internally, she holds court without ceremony. Ministers report to her. Commanders brief her. Her voice shapes internal narratives. And while the Supreme Leader retains his spotlight, it is Yo-jong who prepares the script, controls the lighting, and cues the actors.

The people do not chant her name. But they fear her. Her role in purges is well documented. Her influence in surveillance operations is undeniable. She has signed the death of many with her silence alone.

Still, she is not reckless. Her rule is disciplined, her actions measured. She plays the long game. Where others would demand titles, she allows speculation. Where others would raise flags, she raises questions. The uncertainty around her status is not a weakness—it is a shield.

To the world, she remains an enigma. Is she the next leader? The shadow regent? The power behind the throne? The answer may be all of the above.

She wears no crown. But she has inherited the weight of one.

And in North Korea, that weight is heavier than any gold.

THE HIDDEN EXECUTOR

Death in North Korea does not come from a court ruling or a trial. It comes in whispers, in sealed orders, in nods exchanged in sterile rooms. And often, the hand behind those deaths is not the man in the military uniform—but the woman with a pen. Kim Yo-jong, North Korea's hidden executor, has built a reputation not through spectacle, but through silent elimination.

She does not carry out executions personally. She doesn't need to. Her authority is such that a glance, a signature, or a delayed response can seal the fate of a man who has fallen from grace. Her purges are surgical—precise, timed, and largely invisible to the outside world. They leave no bodies in the streets, only gaps in leadership charts.

Early signs of her lethal reach emerged during the reshuffling of the propaganda and diplomatic arms of the regime. Officials who once held prominence were removed without explanation. New faces, often less ambitious but more loyal, were installed. The message was clear: survival depended not on talent, but on proximity to her trust.

One high-profile case was the rumored execution of a high-ranking official who had failed to properly stage a cultural event meant to impress foreign media. Sources indicated that Yo-jong viewed the failure not just as incompetence, but as ideological sabotage. Within days, the official disappeared.

She does not tolerate embarrassment. She does not forgive weakness.

Internally, her power to execute is tied not to law but to perception. In North Korea, where image is everything, a mistake in messaging is a threat to the state. And Yo-jong is the guardian of the state's image. This makes her the final arbiter of ideological purity—and the enforcer of its consequences.
But her reach goes further.

In matters of diplomacy, she has reportedly ordered the sidelining of entire delegations who failed to impress foreign envoys. In cultural policy, she has purged artists and writers whose work lacked "spirit." Her oversight extends to surveillance as well—those who whisper dissent find themselves silenced, not with trials, but with erasure.

Her execution style is bureaucratic. Files vanish. Names are removed. Biographies are edited. History itself is rewritten to accommodate her decisions.

This method makes her terrifying. Her power is invisible until it's too late. There are no warnings, no second chances. Her face is calm. Her voice is soft. Her decisions, final.

She does not appear in courtrooms.

Because in North Korea, the executor needs no robe.

She only needs to be obeyed.

THE DIGITAL CURTAIN

In the age of surveillance, propaganda is no longer limited to posters and loudspeakers. It flows through cables, pulses through satellites, and seeps into every flickering screen. Kim Yo-jong, having mastered traditional propaganda, turned her gaze to the future. She did not just raise a curtain around her country—she made it digital.

The "Digital Curtain" is North Korea's most ambitious form of isolation and control. It is not a wall, but a membrane—porous when needed, impenetrable when not. Yo-jong spearheaded the modernization of North Korea's information controls, transitioning the regime from analog indoctrination to networked obedience.

Under her supervision, the country's intranet, known as Kwangmyong, expanded in both reach and sophistication. It connects government offices, schools, and selected households, but never to the outside world. It mimics the internet in function, but not in freedom. Every site, every search, every keystroke is monitored. Every byte of content has her ideological fingerprint.

She launched campaigns encouraging digital literacy, all under the guise of national pride. Students were taught programming, graphic design, and even basic AI. But all of it was within a sandbox of state control. No global tools. No external communication. Innovation, but only for internal glory.

At the same time, she cracked down on smuggled USBs, foreign films, and South Korean dramas. Punishments for possession of outside content grew harsher. Informant networks grew larger. Border guards were equipped with tech-sniffing tools. She was not just fighting ideology—she was waging war on data.

But Yo-jong did not ignore the power of optics abroad. She directed the creation of sleek, foreign-facing YouTube channels managed through third parties. These platforms portrayed North Korea as a quirky, misunderstood nation—highlighting markets, singing children, and the "modern life" of citizens. These weren't just propaganda—they were reverse psy-ops, designed to confuse, distract, and dilute criticism.

Her strategy wasn't to block information. It was to replace it.

When global critics highlighted famine, she released videos of rice harvests. When defectors described executions, she aired stories of family reunions. The truth wasn't denied—it was drowned.

She also invested in cyber capability. Under her oversight, cyber units within North Korea's military grew in both size and ambition. They didn't just hack—they harvested. Crypto thefts, ransomware attacks, espionage campaigns—all traced back to units operating under ministries she influenced.

The Digital Curtain became not just a shield, but a weapon.

It protected the regime from ideological contamination.

And it gave Kim Yo-jong the power to shape not just what her people believed, but what the world believed about her people.

In a world ruled by screens, she became the editor of perception.

And in her hands, the truth became programmable.

THE SILENT BUTTON

It's said that the power to destroy the world lies under the control of a single hand. In North Korea, that hand has long been presumed to be Kim Jong-un's. But in the innermost chambers of the regime—where security clearance reaches mythic levels and commands are issued without signatures—a question lingers in whispers: what if the button isn't his alone?

What if it's hers?

Kim Yo-jong, through years of quiet ascent and ruthless consolidation, has come closer to the instruments of annihilation than any woman in North Korea's history. She does not command armies by rank, but she commands them by influence. She does not launch missiles, but she chooses when to show them. And increasingly, she is seen not as a shadow to the Supreme Leader—but as his voice, his strategist, his contingency.

Her proximity to nuclear decisions has been confirmed by defectors and analysts alike. She is present at missile tests. She is briefed on technological advancements. Her statements regarding "final destruction" are not rhetorical flourishes—they are signals. Measured, methodical, chilling.

In 2024, after several joint drills between South Korea and the United States, Yo-jong issued a rare direct threat: any further provocation, she said, would result in "an action that would end all dialogue." Her words were followed by the mobilization of missile units. No further warning was given.

And yet, no launch followed. That restraint was not seen as weakness—it was strategy. Yo-jong had learned that fear multiplies in silence. A button not pushed is more terrifying than one slammed. The unknown, she understood, was the ultimate deterrent.

She represents a shift in how nuclear power is perceived. While male leaders often use it for bluster and visibility, she uses it like a secret—kept quiet, carried close, and revealed only as needed.

Her threat isn't in tantrums or declarations, but in the calmness of her tone.

Her access to military briefings, her involvement in cyber operations, and her increasing authority in strategic decisions have positioned her as the unspoken co-holder of North Korea's most devastating potential. Whether she has the literal codes or not, she has the trust. And in a regime built on personal loyalty, that trust is more potent than any policy.

The button is metaphorical, yes. But it's also real.

And in a regime where silence is power, the world may not hear it click.

Not until it's too late.

TERMINOLOGY AND DICTIONARY

Architect of Soft Power – A title attributed to Kim Yo-jong, referencing her role in shaping North Korea's international image through calculated diplomacy, strategic charm offensives, and manipulative global media campaigns.

Balloon Campaigns – Activist-led missions from South Korea that involve floating balloons over the DMZ (Demilitarized Zone) into North Korea, carrying propaganda leaflets, USBs, or other anti-regime materials.

Crownless Queen – A term used to describe Kim Yo-jong's de facto power within the regime despite holding no official title that reflects her true authority.

Defectors – North Korean citizens who have escaped the country to seek asylum, often in South Korea or the West. They serve as sources of intelligence and testimony on life within the regime.

Demilitarized Zone (DMZ) – The heavily fortified border separating North and South Korea. It is both a symbolic and literal frontier of military tension and ideological division.

Digital Curtain – Kim Yo-jong's modernization of North Korea's surveillance and censorship infrastructure, designed to isolate its people from foreign information and project a state-controlled digital reality.

First Lady of Fear – A descriptor reflecting Kim Yo-jong's emergence as the regime's most feared operator, overseeing purges and executing internal power plays with calm ruthlessness.

Hidden Executor – A title referencing Kim Yo-jong's role in ordering and authorizing purges, disappearances, and executions within the North Korean elite through indirect and untraceable means.

Intranet (Kwangmyong) – North Korea's internal network, controlled and firewalled from the global internet. Used for propaganda, education, and government communication.

Juche – The official state ideology of North Korea, emphasizing self-reliance, nationalism, and the absolute authority of the ruling Kim family.

Kim Il-sung – Founder of North Korea and grandfather of Kim Yo-jong. He established the ruling dynasty and remains an eternal figurehead in state propaganda.

Kim Jong-il – Father of Kim Yo-jong and Kim Jong-un. Ruled North Korea from 1994 until his death in 2011. Known for deepening the regime's isolation and cult of personality.

Kim Jong-un – Supreme Leader of North Korea and brother to Kim Yo-jong. Assumed power after their father's death and is publicly regarded as the nation's ultimate authority.

Kim Yo-jong – Central figure of this book. Sister to Kim Jong-un, she evolved from a shadowy presence to the regime's key political strategist, propagandist, and power broker.

Ko Yong-hui – Consort to Kim Jong-il and mother of Kim Yo-jong. Her Japanese heritage was politically sensitive within the regime.

Ko Yong-suk (Aunt Ko) – Sister of Ko Yong-hui and caretaker of the Kim siblings during their education in Switzerland. Later defected to the United States, offering testimony on the siblings' upbringing.

Kwangmyong – See Intranet. A state-controlled network used in lieu of the open internet within North Korea.

Liaison Office (Kaesong) – A now-destroyed diplomatic hub that served as a rare symbol of cooperation between North and South Korea. Its demolition, ordered by Kim Yo-jong, marked a major regression in inter-Korean relations.

Media Strategist – A title referencing Kim Yo-jong's reformation of North Korea's domestic and foreign-facing media, enhancing its sophistication to influence both internal loyalty and external perception.

Olympic Debut (2018 Winter Olympics) – Refers to Kim Yo-jong's first major public appearance on the international stage during the Pyeongchang Games, which introduced her as a diplomatic actor.

PAD (Propaganda and Agitation Department) – A critical agency within the Korean Workers' Party responsible for all ideological messaging, media, and cultural control. Kim Yo-jong held significant authority here.

Puppets and Strings – A metaphor describing Kim Yo-jong's behind-the-scenes control over party officials and ministries, despite not holding overt leadership titles.

Putin's Pact – Refers to the military and economic agreement between North Korea and Russia in 2024. Brokered during a summit involving Kim Jong-un and Vladimir Putin, with orchestration by Kim Yo-jong.

Silent Button – A metaphor symbolizing the unspoken but perceived authority Kim Yo-jong holds over North Korea's nuclear command infrastructure.

Soft Edge of a Hard Regime – A phrase describing Kim Yo-jong's strategy to soften North Korea's global image without altering its authoritarian structure.

Subtle Erasure – A term denoting Kim Yo-jong's method of executing purges not through public trials but via disappearances, historical rewrites, and bureaucratic vanishing acts.

Supreme Leader – Title held by the reigning head of state in North Korea, currently Kim Jong-un.

Swiss Secret – Refers to the covert schooling of Kim Yo-jong and Kim Jong-un in Switzerland under false identities during the 1990s.

The Castle on the Horizon – A poetic image used to symbolize the fantasy of a normal childhood for the Kim siblings while visiting Disneyland Paris—a rare glimpse of innocence overshadowed by destiny.

War of Optics – A concept denoting the regime's shift toward influencing foreign perception through calculated imagery, diplomacy, and curated messaging rather than direct confrontation.

Printed by Libri Plureos GmbH in Hamburg,
Germany

9 798231 071906